First Name:

Last Name:

Address:

Company:

Email:

Mobile:

Phone:

Certification Name:

Certification Exam Prep Notebook #:

Exam Date:

Notebook Start Date:

Notebook Finish Date:

If lost, please return to:

Reward:

D1532714

Table of Contents

MONTHLY PLANNER

_____

_____

_____

_____

	Monday	Tuesday	Wednesday	Thursday	Friday	Saturday	Sunday
	JANUARY						
Week52							
Week1							
Week2							
Week3							
Week4							

FEBRUARY

	Monday	Tuesday	Wednesday	Thursday	Friday	Saturday	Sunday
Week 5							
Week 6							
Week 7							
Week 8							

	MARCH					
	Monday	Tuesday	Wednesday	Thursday	Friday	Saturday	Sunday
Week 9							
Week 10							
Week 11							
Week 12							
Week 13							

APRIL

	Monday	Tuesday	Wednesday	Thursday	Friday	Saturday	Sunday
Week 13							
Week 14							
Week 15							
Week 16							
Week 17							

MAY

	Monday	Tuesday	Wednesday	Thursday	Friday	Saturday	Sunday
Week 17							
Week 18							
Week 19							
Week 20							
Week 21							
Week 22							

	JUNE					
Monday	Tuesday	Wednesday	Thursday	Friday	Saturday	Sunday
Week 22						
Week 23						
Week 24						
Week 25						
Week 26						

	Monday	Tuesday	Wednesday	Thursday	Friday	Saturday	Sunday
	JULY						
Week 26							
Week 27							
Week 28							
Week 29							
Week 30							

AUGUST

	Monday	Tuesday	Wednesday	Thursday	Friday	Saturday	Sunday
Week 30							
Week 31							
Week 32							
Week 33							
Week 34							
Week 35							

SEPTEMBER

	Monday	Tuesday	Wednesday	Thursday	Friday	Saturday	Sunday
Week 35							
Week 36							
Week 37							
Week 38							
Week 39							

OCTOBER

	Monday	Tuesday	Wednesday	Thursday	Friday	Saturday	Sunday
Week 39							
Week 40							
Week 41							
Week 42							
Week 43							

NOVEMBER

	Monday	Tuesday	Wednesday	Thursday	Friday	Saturday	Sunday
Week 44							
Week 45							
Week 46							
Week 47							
Week 48							

DECEMBER

	Monday	Tuesday	Wednesday	Thursday	Friday	Saturday	Sunday
Week 48							
Week 49							
Week 50							
Week 51							
Week 52							

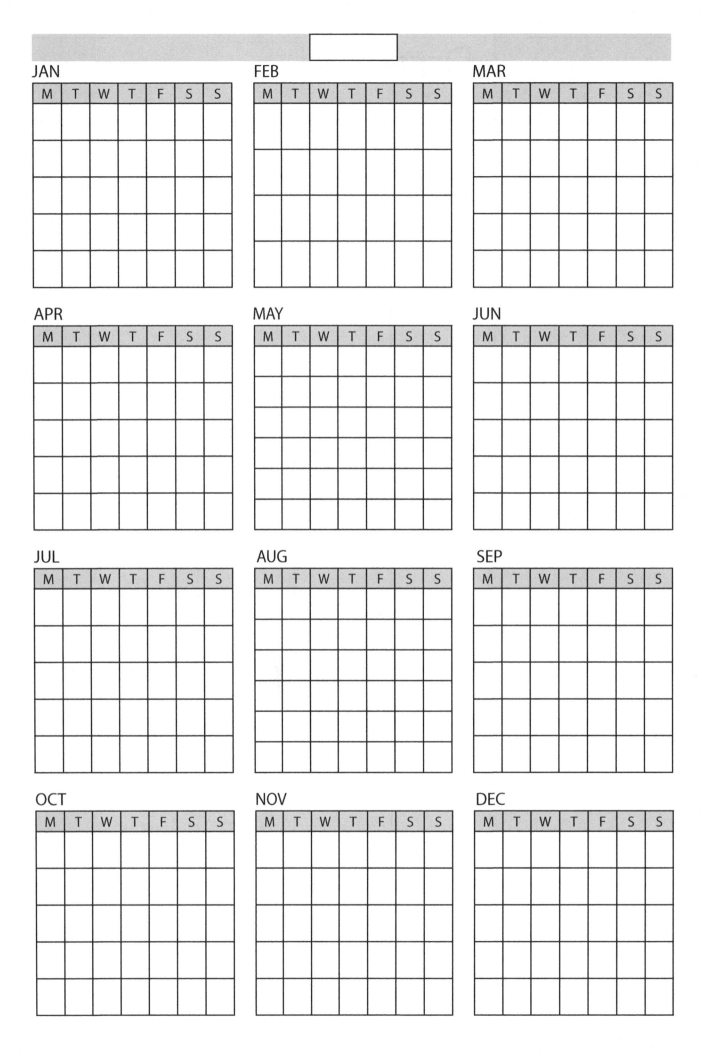

STUDY PLAN TIMELINE

Exam Study Plan Timeline

Wk#	Day	Exam Prep Activities					Hours	☑
Wk1	**1-4**	Complete _____ Exam Prep Course					Ph:	S ☐
		Classroom ☐ Online ☐ Self-Paced ☐		☐		☐	Ah:	F ☐
Wk2	**1**	e.g. Review ECO/ES Topic:					Ph:	S ☐
		e.g. Guide ☐	☐	☐	☐	☐	Ah:	F ☐
Wk2	**2**						Ph:	S ☐
		☐	☐	☐	☐	☐	Ah:	F ☐
Wk2	**3**						Ph:	S ☐
		☐	☐	☐	☐	☐	Ah:	F ☐
Wk2	**4**						Ph:	S ☐
		☐	☐	☐	☐	☐	Ah:	F ☐
Wk2	**5**						Ph:	S ☐
		☐	☐	☐	☐	☐	Ah:	F ☐
Wk2	**6**						Ph:	S ☐
		☐	☐	☐	☐	☐	Ah:	F ☐
Wk3	**1**						Ph:	S ☐
		☐	☐	☐	☐	☐	Ah:	F ☐
Wk3	**2**						Ph:	S ☐
		☐	☐	☐	☐	☐	Ah:	F ☐
Wk3	**3**						Ph:	S ☐
		☐	☐	☐	☐	☐	Ah:	F ☐
Wk3	**4**						Ph:	S ☐
		☐	☐	☐	☐	☐	Ah:	F ☐
Wk3	**5**						Ph:	S ☐
		☐	☐	☐	☐	☐	Ah:	F ☐
Wk3	**6**						Ph:	S ☐
		☐	☐	☐	☐	☐	Ah:	F ☐

Note: S - Started; F - Finished; P - Passed the exam; Ph - Planned study hours; Ah - Actual study hours; ECO - Exam Content Outline; ES - Exam Specfication.

Wk#	Day	Exam Prep Activities					Hours	☑
Wk4	1						Ph:	S ☐
		☐	☐	☐	☐	☐	Ah:	F ☐
Wk4	2						Ph:	S ☐
		☐	☐	☐	☐	☐	Ah:	F ☐
Wk4	3						Ph:	S ☐
		☐	☐	☐	☐	☐	Ah:	F ☐
Wk4	4						Ph:	S ☐
		☐	☐	☐	☐	☐	Ah:	F ☐
Wk4	5						Ph:	S ☐
		☐	☐	☐	☐	☐	Ah:	F ☐
Wk4	6						Ph:	S ☐
		☐	☐	☐	☐	☐	Ah:	F ☐
Wk4	7						Ph:	S ☐
		☐	☐	☐	☐	☐	Ah:	F ☐
Wk5	1						Ph:	S ☐
		☐	☐	☐	☐	☐	Ah:	F ☐
Wk5	2						Ph:	S ☐
		☐	☐	☐	☐	☐	Ah:	F ☐
Wk5	3						Ph:	S ☐
		☐	☐	☐	☐	☐	Ah:	F ☐
Wk5	4						Ph:	S ☐
		☐	☐	☐	☐	☐	Ah:	F ☐
Wk5	5						Ph:	S ☐
		☐	☐	☐	☐	☐	Ah:	F ☐
Wk5	6						Ph:	S ☐
		☐	☐	☐	☐	☐	Ah:	F ☐
Wk5	7						Ph:	S ☐
		☐	☐	☐	☐	☐	Ah:	F ☐

Wk#	Day	Exam Prep Activities						Hours	☑
Wk6	1							Ph:	S ☐
			☐	☐	☐	☐	☐	Ah:	F ☐
Wk6	2							Ph:	S ☐
			☐	☐	☐	☐	☐	Ah:	F ☐
Wk6	3							Ph:	S ☐
			☐	☐	☐	☐	☐	Ah:	F ☐
Wk6	4							Ph:	S ☐
			☐	☐	☐	☐	☐	Ah:	F ☐
Wk6	5							Ph:	S ☐
			☐	☐	☐	☐	☐	Ah:	F ☐
Wk6	6							Ph:	S ☐
			☐	☐	☐	☐	☐	Ah:	F ☐
Wk6	7							Ph:	S ☐
			☐	☐	☐	☐	☐	Ah:	F ☐
Wk7	1							Ph:	S ☐
			☐	☐	☐	☐	☐	Ah:	F ☐
Wk7	2							Ph:	S ☐
			☐	☐	☐	☐	☐	Ah:	F ☐
Wk7	3							Ph:	S ☐
			☐	☐	☐	☐	☐	Ah:	F ☐
Wk7	4							Ph:	S ☐
			☐	☐	☐	☐	☐	Ah:	F ☐
Wk7	5	Take Mock Exam Set #1						Ph: Ah:	S☐ F☐
		Review Mock Exam Set #1 Incorrect answers						Ph: Ah:	S☐ F☐
Wk7	6	Take Mock Exam Set #2						Ph: Ah:	S☐ F☐
		Review Mock Exam Set #2 Incorrect answers						Ph: Ah:	S☐ F☐
Exam	___	Day before the exam, do not study anything!						0	
Wk__	___	Exam Day! - Successfully pass the exam! You can do it!						_____	P ☐

Wk#	Day	Exam Prep Activities/Topics	Hours	☑
				☐
				☐
				☐
				☐
				☐
				☐
				☐
				☐
				☐
				☐
				☐
				☐
				☐
				☐
				☐
				☐
				☐
				☐
				☐
				☐
				☐
				☐
				☐
				☐
				☐
				☐

Exam Study Plan Timeline - Custom

Wk#	Day	Exam Prep Activities/Topics	Hours	☑

Exam Study Plan Timeline - Custom

Wk#	Day	Exam Prep Activities/Topics	Hours	☑
				☐
				☐
				☐
				☐
				☐
				☐
				☐
				☐
				☐
				☐
				☐
				☐
				☐
				☐
				☐
				☐
				☐
				☐
				☐
				☐
				☐
				☐
				☐
				☐
				☐
				☐
				☐
Wk#	Day	Exam Prep Activities/Topics	Hours	☐

Exam Study Plan Timeline - Custom

Wk#	Day	Exam Prep Activities/Topics	Hours	☑
				☐
				☐
				☐
				☐
				☐
				☐
				☐
				☐
				☐
				☐
				☐
				☐
				☐
				☐
				☐
				☐
				☐
				☐
				☐
				☐
				☐
				☐

Exam Study Plan Timeline - Custom

Wk#	Day	Exam Prep Activities/Topics	Hours	☑

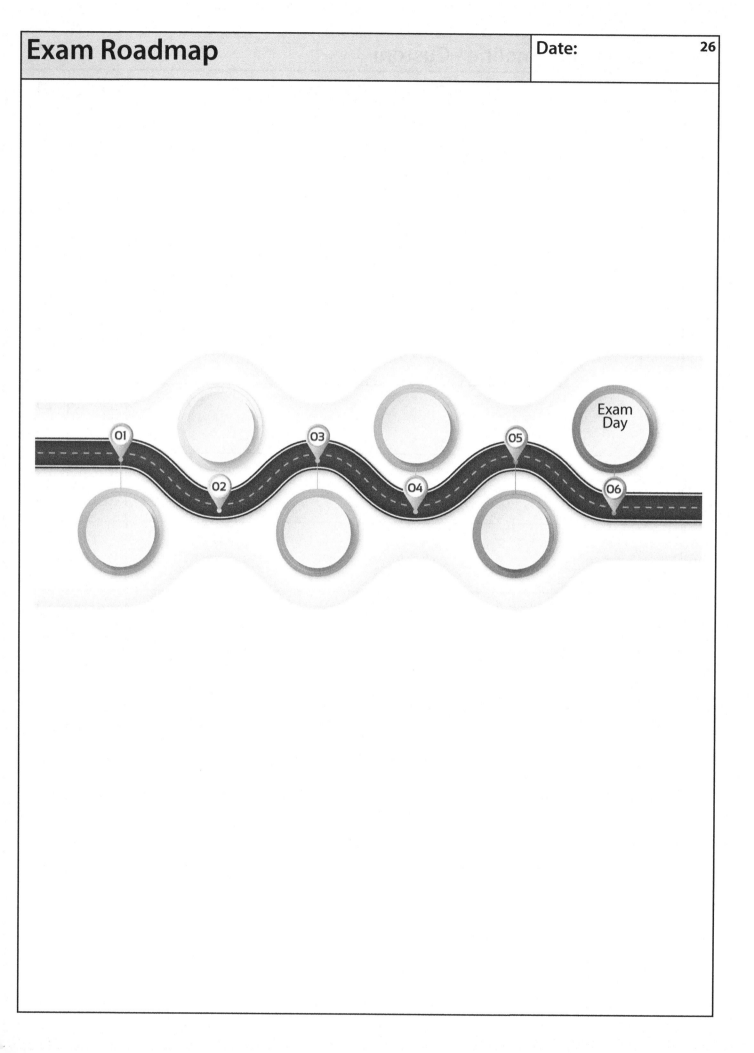

Various Steps (Refer exam website for the latest requirements)

Professional Experience + Degree Requirements		
Training Hours Requirements		
Exam Application Submission		
Register for Exam		
Exam Preparation & Take Exam		

REFERENCE

STUDY

MATERIALS

No.	Description	Author/Publisher/Web	Edition	Book/eBook
	Exam Prep Books			
	_____ Books			

Exam Reference Study Materials

Exam Reference Study Materials

No.	Description	Author/Website	Edition	Book/eBook
	Exam Guide book/Frameworks/Standards			
	Mock Exam Resources			

Exam Reference Study Materials

No.	Description			

Exam Reference Study Materials

No.	Description			

Exam Online Resources Login Information

Website		Website	
Username		Username	
Password		Password	
Notes		Notes	
Website		Website	
Username		Username	
Password		Password	
Notes		Notes	
Website		Website	
Username		Username	
Password		Password	
Notes		Notes	
Website		Website	
Username		Username	
Password		Password	
Notes		Notes	
Website		Website	
Username		Username	
Password		Password	
Notes		Notes	
Website		Website	
Username		Username	
Password		Password	
Notes		Notes	
Website		Website	
Username		Username	
Password		Password	
Notes		Notes	

Exam Online Resources Login Information

Website		Website	
Username		Username	
Password		Password	
Notes		Notes	
Website		Website	
Username		Username	
Password		Password	
Notes		Notes	
Website		Website	
Username		Username	
Password		Password	
Notes		Notes	
Website		Website	
Username		Username	
Password		Password	
Notes		Notes	
Website		Website	
Username		Username	
Password		Password	
Notes		Notes	
Website		Website	
Username		Username	
Password		Password	
Notes		Notes	
Website		Website	
Username		Username	
Password		Password	
Notes		Notes	

WEEKLY STUDY PLANNER

ECO - EXAM CONTENT OUTLINE/ ES - EXAM SPECIFICATION
ECS/ES #1/#2: HELPS TO CROSS REFERENCE THE TOPIC (S) TO THE EXAM
OFFICIAL ECO/ES.

Week #/ Day #	ECO/ES#1	ECS/ES#2	EXAM TOPICS 38	Started	Finished	Reviewed	Page #
				○ ○	○ ○	○ ○	
				○ ○	○ ○	○ ○	
				○ ○	○ ○	○ ○	
				○ ○	○ ○	○ ○	
				○ ○	○ ○	○ ○	
				○ ○	○ ○	○ ○	
				○ ○	○ ○	○ ○	
				○ ○	○ ○	○ ○	
				○ ○	○ ○	○ ○	
				○ ○	○ ○	○ ○	
				○ ○	○ ○	○ ○	
				○ ○	○ ○	○ ○	
				○ ○	○ ○	○ ○	
				○ ○	○ ○	○ ○	
			EXAM TOPICS 38	○ ○	○ ○	○ ○	Page #

Week #/ Day #	ECO/ES#1	ECS/ES#2 ___	EXAM TOPICS 39	Started	Finished	Reviewed	Page #
				○	○	○	
.....	.....	.....		○	○	○	
				○	○	○	
.....	.....	.....		○	○	○	
				○	○	○	
.....	.....	.....		○	○	○	
				○	○	○	
.....	.....	.....		○	○	○	
				○	○	○	
.....	.....	.....		○	○	○	
				○	○	○	
.....	.....	.....		○	○	○	
				○	○	○	
.....	.....	.....		○	○	○	
				○	○	○	
.....	.....	.....		○	○	○	
				○	○	○	
.....	.....	.....		○	○	○	
				○	○	○	
.....	.....	.....		○	○	○	
				○	○	○	
.....	.....	.....		○	○	○	
				○	○	○	
.....	.....	.....		○	○	○	
				○	○	○	
.....	.....	.....		○	○	○	
			EXAM TOPICS 39	○	○	○	
.....	.....	.....		○	○	○	

Week #/ Day #	ECO/ES#1	ECS/ES#2 ___	EXAM TOPICS	40	STARTED	FINISHED	REVIEWED	PAGE #
					○	○	○	
					○	○	○	
					○	○	○	
					○	○	○	
					○	○	○	
					○	○	○	
					○	○	○	
					○	○	○	
					○	○	○	
					○	○	○	
					○	○	○	
					○	○	○	
					○	○	○	
					○	○	○	
					○	○	○	
					○	○	○	
					○	○	○	
					○	○	○	
					○	○	○	
					○	○	○	
					○	○	○	
					○	○	○	
					○	○	○	
					○	○	○	
					○	○	○	
					○	○	○	
			EXAM TOPICS		○	○	○	
					○	○	○	

Week #/ Day #	ECO/ES#1	ECS/ES#2	EXAM TOPICS 41	Started	Finished	Reviewed	Page #
				○	○	○	
				○	○	○	
				○	○	○	
				○	○	○	
				○	○	○	
				○	○	○	
				○	○	○	
				○	○	○	
				○	○	○	
				○	○	○	
				○	○	○	
				○	○	○	
				○	○	○	
				○	○	○	
				○	○	○	
				○	○	○	
				○	○	○	
				○	○	○	
				○	○	○	
				○	○	○	
				○	○	○	
				○	○	○	
				○	○	○	
				○	○	○	
				○	○	○	
				○	○	○	
	ECO/ES#1	ECS/ES#2		○	○	○	

Week #/ Day #	ECO/ES#1	ECS/ES#2	EXAM TOPICS 42	Started	Finished	Reviewed	Page #
				○	○	○	
				○	○	○	
				○	○	○	
				○	○	○	
				○	○	○	
				○	○	○	
				○	○	○	
				○	○	○	
				○	○	○	
				○	○	○	
				○	○	○	
				○	○	○	
				○	○	○	
				○	○	○	
				○	○	○	
				○	○	○	
				○	○	○	
				○	○	○	
				○	○	○	
				○	○	○	
				○	○	○	
				○	○	○	
				○	○	○	
				○	○	○	
				○	○	○	
				○	○	○	
				○	○	○	
				○	○	○	

Week #/ Day #	ECO/ES#1	ECS/ES#2 ___	EXAM TOPICS 43	Started	Finished	Reviewed	Page #
				○	○	○	
				○	○	○	
				○	○	○	
				○	○	○	
				○	○	○	
				○	○	○	
				○	○	○	
				○	○	○	
				○	○	○	
				○	○	○	
				○	○	○	
				○	○	○	
				○	○	○	
				○	○	○	
				○	○	○	
				○	○	○	
				○	○	○	
				○	○	○	
				○	○	○	
				○	○	○	
				○	○	○	
				○	○	○	
				○	○	○	
				○	○	○	
				○	○	○	
				○	○	○	
				○	○	○	
				○	○	○	
				○	○	○	
				○	○	○	
				○	○	○	
				○	○	○	

Week #/ Day #	ECO/ES#1	ECS/ES#2	EXAM TOPICS 44	Started	Finished	Reviewed	Page #
				○	○	○	
				○	○	○	
				○	○	○	
				○	○	○	
				○	○	○	
				○	○	○	
				○	○	○	
				○	○	○	
				○	○	○	
				○	○	○	
				○	○	○	
				○	○	○	
				○	○	○	
				○	○	○	
				○	○	○	
				○	○	○	
				○	○	○	
				○	○	○	
				○	○	○	
				○	○	○	
				○	○	○	
				○	○	○	
				○	○	○	
				○	○	○	
				○	○	○	
				○	○	○	
				○	○	○	
				○	○	○	
				○	○	○	
ECO/ES#1	ECS/ES#2			○	○	○	
				○	○	○	

Week #/ Day #	ECO/ES#1	ECS/ES#2 ___	EXAM TOPICS 45	Started	Finished	Reviewed	Page #
				○	○	○	
				○	○	○	
				○	○	○	
				○	○	○	
				○	○	○	
				○	○	○	
				○	○	○	
				○	○	○	
				○	○	○	
				○	○	○	
				○	○	○	
				○	○	○	
				○	○	○	
				○	○	○	
				○	○	○	
				○	○	○	
				○	○	○	
				○	○	○	
				○	○	○	
				○	○	○	
				○	○	○	
				○	○	○	
				○	○	○	
				○	○	○	
				○	○	○	
				○	○	○	
				○	○	○	
				○	○	○	

Week #/ Day #	ECO/ES#1	ECS/ES#2	EXAM TOPICS 46	Started	Finished	Reviewed	Page #
				○	○	○	
				○	○	○	
				○	○	○	
				○	○	○	
				○	○	○	
				○	○	○	
				○	○	○	
				○	○	○	
				○	○	○	
				○	○	○	
				○	○	○	
				○	○	○	
				○	○	○	
				○	○	○	
				○	○	○	
				○	○	○	
				○	○	○	
				○	○	○	
				○	○	○	
				○	○	○	
				○	○	○	
				○	○	○	
				○	○	○	
				○	○	○	
				○	○	○	
				○	○	○	
				○	○	○	
				○	○	○	
				○	○	○	
				○	○	○	
				○	○	○	
				○	○	○	

Week #/ Day #	ECO/ES#1	ECS/ES#2	EXAM TOPICS 47	STARTED	FINISHED	REVIEWED	PAGE #
				○	○	○	
				○	○	○	
				○	○	○	
				○	○	○	
				○	○	○	
				○	○	○	
				○	○	○	
				○	○	○	
				○	○	○	
				○	○	○	
				○	○	○	
				○	○	○	
				○	○	○	
				○	○	○	
				○	○	○	
				○	○	○	
				○	○	○	
				○	○	○	
				○	○	○	
				○	○	○	
				○	○	○	
				○	○	○	
				○	○	○	
				○	○	○	
				○	○	○	
				○	○	○	
				○	○	○	
				○	○	○	
				○	○	○	
Week #/ Day #	ECO/ES#1	ECS/ES#2		STARTED	FINISHED	REVIEWED	PAGE #

Week #/ Day #	ECO/ES#1	ECS/ES#2	EXAM TOPICS 48	Started	Finished	Reviewed	Page #
				○ ○	○ ○	○ ○	
				○ ○	○ ○	○ ○	
				○ ○	○ ○	○ ○	
				○ ○	○ ○	○ ○	
				○ ○	○ ○	○ ○	
				○ ○	○ ○	○ ○	
				○ ○	○ ○	○ ○	
				○ ○	○ ○	○ ○	
				○ ○	○ ○	○ ○	
				○ ○	○ ○	○ ○	
				○ ○	○ ○	○ ○	
				○ ○	○ ○	○ ○	
				○ ○	○ ○	○ ○	
				○ ○	○ ○	○ ○	
ECO/ES#1	ECS/ES#2			○ ○	○ ○	○ ○	

CORNELL NOTE TAKING

Cornell Note-Taking Instruction Page

Exam Topic: Write the exam topic from the Exam Content Outline (ECO)/Exam Specification (ES)	**Date:** M T W T F S S	50

Main Cues:	Main Notes:
When to use: Written briefly after lecture/ exam prep class or textbook reading.	**When to use:** Notes taking during lecture/exam prep class or textbook reading.
Contents:	**Contents:**
* Main ideas & key concepts, topic keywords	* Main ideas and concepts - Concise sentences
* Vocabulary	* Paraphrase
* Questions answered by Main notes	* Bullet points/lists
* Main phrases	* Charts/diagrams
* Exam study prompts	* Abbreviations
* Key questions for course instructor	* Formulas
* Important facts	
* Anticipated Exam questions	
	Tips:
	* Leave space between sentences/topics/ideas
	* Cut unnecessary words
Anticipated Exam Questions:	* Use telegraphic sentences
	* Abbreviate familiar words
	* Not formal outlines

Summary: **When to use:** Write after the lecture/exam prep class or textbook reading. Review the summary regularly.
☐ **Contents:**
☐   * Brief summary of notes highlighting main notes/points on the page.
☐   * Five most important points of the topic/lecture/chapter.
☐   * Questions still need to answer.
☐

Exam Topic: Write the exam topic from the Exam Content Outline (ECO)/Exam Specification (ES)	**Date:** M T W T F S S	51

When to use:	**When to use:**
* During the lecture/exam prep class or textbook reading.	* After the lecture/exam prep class or textbook reading. During review.
* Write down the main notes that are specific to the exam topic.	* Write down the main notes that are specific to the exam topic.

Summary:		References	References
When to use: Write after the lecture/exam prep class or textbook reading. Review the summary regularly.		**When to use:**	
Contents:		During the lecture/exam prep class or textbook reading	After the lecture/exam prep class or textbook reading
* Brief summary of notes highlighting main notes/points on the page.		Write the guide's chapter#/section # with page# for quick references.	Write the guide's chapter#/section # with page# for quick references.
* Questions still need to answer.			

Exam Topic:

Main Cues:	Main Notes:
Anticipated Exam Questions:	

Summary:

- [ ]
- [ ]
- [ ]
- [ ]
- [ ]

Exam Topic:

Summary:	References	References

Exam Topic:

Main Cues:	Main Notes:
Anticipated Exam Questions:	

Summary:

☐

☐

☐

☐

☐

Exam Topic:

Summary:

	References	References

Exam Topic:

Exam Topic:

Main Cues:	Main Notes:

Anticipated Exam Questions:

Summary:

- [ ]
- [ ]
- [ ]
- [ ]
- [ ]

Exam Topic:

Date:

M T W T F S S

Summary:	References	References

Exam Topic:	Date: 58
	M T W T F S S

Main Cues:	Main Notes:
Anticipated Exam Questions:	

Summary:

☐

☐

☐

☐

☐

Exam Topic:

Date:
M T W T F S S

Summary:	References	References

| Exam Topic: | Date: 60 |
| | M T W T F S S |

Main Cues:	Main Notes:
Anticipated Exam Questions:	

Summary:

- [ ]
- [ ]
- [ ]
- [ ]
- [ ]

Exam Topic:

Date:

M T W T F S S

Summary:	References	References

Exam Topic:

Main Cues:	Main Notes:
Anticipated Exam Questions:	

Summary:

☐

☐

☐

☐

☐

Exam Topic:

Summary:	References	References

Exam Topic:

Main Cues:	Main Notes:
Anticipated Exam Questions:	

Summary:
☐
☐
☐
☐
☐

Summary:

References	References

Exam Topic:

Main Cues:	Main Notes:

Anticipated Exam Questions:	

Summary:

☐

☐

☐

☐

☐

Exam Topic:

Date:

M T W T F S S

Summary:	References	References

Exam Topic: Date: 68

Main Cues:	Main Notes:
Anticipated Exam Questions:	

Summary:

- ☐
- ☐
- ☐
- ☐
- ☐

Main Cues:	Main Notes:

Exam Topic:

Date:
M T W T F S S

Summary:	References	References

Exam Topic:

Main Cues:	Main Notes:
Anticipated Exam Questions:	

Summary:

☐

☐

☐

☐

☐

Exam Topic:

Date: 71

M   T   W   T   F   S   S

Summary:

	References	References

Exam Topic:

Main Cues:	Main Notes:

Anticipated Exam Questions:	

Summary:

- ☐
- ☐
- ☐
- ☐
- ☐

Exam Topic:

Summary:	References	References

Exam Topic: **Date:**   74
                                                                   M T W T F S S

Main Cues:	Main Notes:
Anticipated Exam Questions:	

Summary:

☐
☐
☐
☐
☐

Exam Topic:

Summary:	References	References

Exam Topic:

Main Cues:	Main Notes:
Anticipated Exam Questions:	

Summary:

☐

☐

☐

☐

☐

Exam Topic:

Date:
M T W T F S S

Summary:	References	References

Exam Topic:

Main Cues:	Main Notes:

Anticipated Exam Questions:	

Summary:

- ☐
- ☐
- ☐
- ☐
- ☐

Exam Topic:

Date:
M T W T F S S

Summary:	References	References

| Exam Topic: | Date: 80 |
| | M T W T F S S |

Main Cues:	Main Notes:
Anticipated Exam Questions:	

Summary:

- ☐
- ☐
- ☐
- ☐
- ☐

Exam Topic:

Summary:	References	References

Exam Topic:

Date:
M T W T F S S

Main Cues:	Main Notes:
Anticipated Exam Questions:	

Summary:

☐
☐
☐
☐
☐

Exam Topic:

Date:

M T W T F S S

Summary:	References	References

Exam Topic:

Main Cues:	Main Notes:
Anticipated Exam Questions:	

Summary:

- ☐
- ☐
- ☐
- ☐
- ☐

Exam Topic:

Date:

M T W T F S S

Summary:	References	References

Exam Topic:

Main Cues:	Main Notes:
Anticipated Exam Questions:	

Summary:

- ☐
- ☐
- ☐
- ☐
- ☐

Exam Topic:

Summary:	References	References

Exam Topic:

Main Cues:	Main Notes:

Anticipated Exam Questions:	

Summary:

☐

☐

☐

☐

☐

Summary:

	References	References

| Exam Topic: | Date: 90 |
| | M T W T F S S |

Main Cues:	Main Notes:
Anticipated Exam Questions:	

Summary:

- [ ]
- [ ]
- [ ]
- [ ]
- [ ]

Exam Topic:

Date: 91
M T W T F S S

Summary:	References	References

Exam Topic:

Main Cues:	Main Notes:
Anticipated Exam Questions:	

Summary:

- ☐
- ☐
- ☐
- ☐
- ☐

Exam Topic:

Summary:	References	References

Exam Topic:

Date:
M T W T F S S

Main Cues:	Main Notes:
Anticipated Exam Questions:	

Summary:

☐

☐

☐

☐

☐

Exam Topic:

Date: 95

M T W T F S S

Summary:	References	References

Exam Topic:

Main Cues:	Main Notes:

Anticipated Exam Questions:	

Summary:

- ☐
- ☐
- ☐
- ☐
- ☐

Exam Topic:

Date: 97

M T W T F S S

Summary:

Summary:	References	References

Exam Topic:

Main Cues:	Main Notes:
Anticipated Exam Questions:	

Summary:

- [ ]
- [ ]
- [ ]
- [ ]
- [ ]

Exam Topic:

Date:

M T W T F S S

Summary:	References	References

| Exam Topic: | Date: 100 |
| | M T W T F S S |

Main Cues:

Main Notes:

Anticipated Exam Questions:

Summary:

☐

☐

☐

☐

☐

Exam Topic:		Date: 101
		M T W T F S S

Summary:	References	References

Exam Topic:

Main Cues:	Main Notes:
Anticipated Exam Questions:	

Summary:

- [ ]
- [ ]
- [ ]
- [ ]
- [ ]

Exam Topic:

Summary:	References	References
		M T W T F S S

Exam Topic:	Date:	104

Main Cues:	Main Notes:

Anticipated Exam Questions:	

Summary:

- [ ]
- [ ]
- [ ]
- [ ]
- [ ]

Summary:	References	References

Main Cues:

Main Notes:

Anticipated Exam Questions:

Summary:

- ☐
- ☐
- ☐
- ☐
- ☐

Main Cues:

Main Notes:

Exam Topic:

Date:

M T W T F S S

Summary:

	References	References
		M T W T F S S

Main Cues:	Main Notes:
Anticipated Exam Questions:	

Summary:

- ☐
- ☐
- ☐
- ☐
- ☐

Exam Topic:

Summary:	References	References

Exam Topic:

Main Cues:	Main Notes:
Anticipated Exam Questions:	

Summary:

- [ ]
- [ ]
- [ ]
- [ ]
- [ ]

Exam Topic:	Date: 111 M T W T F S S

Summary:	References	References

Exam Topic:

Date:

M T W T F S S

Main Cues:	Main Notes:

Anticipated Exam Questions:	

Summary:

☐

☐

☐

☐

☐

Exam Topic:

Date: 113

M T W T F S S

Summary:	References	References

Exam Topic:

Date:
M T W T F S S

Main Cues:	Main Notes:

Anticipated Exam Questions:

Summary:

☐

☐

☐

☐

☐

Exam Topic:

Date:

M T W T F S S

Summary:

References	References

Exam Topic:

M T W T F S S

Exam Topic:

Main Cues:	Main Notes:
Anticipated Exam Questions:	

Summary:

- [ ]
- [ ]
- [ ]
- [ ]
- [ ]

Exam Topic:

Date: 117

M T W T F S S

Summary:	References	References
		M T W T F S S

Exam Topic:

Main Cues:

Main Notes:

Anticipated Exam Questions:

Summary:

☐

☐

☐

☐

☐

Exam Topic:

Summary:

	References	References
	M T W F S S	

Exam Topic:	Date: 120
	M T W T F S S

Main Cues:	Main Notes:
Anticipated Exam Questions:	

Summary:

☐

☐

☐

☐

☐

Exam Topic:

Summary:	References	References
		M T W F S S

Exam Topic:

Main Cues:	Main Notes:
Anticipated Exam Questions:	

Summary:

- ☐
- ☐
- ☐
- ☐
- ☐

Exam Topic:	Date:	123
	M T W T F S S	

Summary:	References	References

Exam Topic:

Main Cues:	Main Notes:
Anticipated Exam Questions:	

Summary:

- ☐
- ☐
- ☐
- ☐
- ☐

Exam Topic:

Summary:	References	References

Exam Topic:

Main Cues:	Main Notes:

Anticipated Exam Questions:	

Summary:

- [ ]
- [ ]
- [ ]
- [ ]
- [ ]

Exam Topic:

Date:

M T W T F S S

Summary:

References	References

Exam Topic:

Date:

M T W T F S S

Exam Topic:

Main Cues:	Main Notes:

Anticipated Exam Questions:	

Summary:

- ☐
- ☐
- ☐
- ☐
- ☐

Exam Topic:

Summary:	References	References

Exam Topic:

Main Cues:	Main Notes:

Anticipated Exam Questions:	

Summary:

- [ ]
- [ ]
- [ ]
- [ ]
- [ ]

Exam Topic:

Date:
M T W T F S S

Summary:	References	References

Exam Topic:

Date:
M T W T F S S

Main Cues:	Main Notes:
Anticipated Exam Questions:	

Summary:

- [ ]
- [ ]
- [ ]
- [ ]
- [ ]

Exam Topic:

Date:

M T W T F S S

Summary:

	References	References

Exam Topic:

Date:

M T W T F S S

Main Cues:

Main Notes:

Anticipated Exam Questions:

Summary:

☐

☐

☐

☐

☐

Exam Topic:

Summary:	References	References

Exam Topic:

Main Cues:	Main Notes:
Anticipated Exam Questions:	

Summary:

- [ ]
- [ ]
- [ ]
- [ ]
- [ ]

Exam Topic:

Date:

M T W T F S S

Summary:	References	References

Exam Topic:

Date: 138

M T W T F S S

Main Cues:	Main Notes:

Anticipated Exam Questions:	

Summary:

☐

☐

☐

☐

☐

Exam Topic:

Summary:	References	References

Exam Topic:

| Exam Topic: | Date: 140 |
| | M T W T F S S |

Main Cues:	Main Notes:
Anticipated Exam Questions:	

Summary:

- ☐
- ☐
- ☐
- ☐
- ☐

Exam Topic:

Date:

M T W T F S S

Summary:	References	References

EXAM WORKOUT SHEETS

Important Contacts

Name	Email	in ⓘ f 🐦	Phone/Cell

Important Contacts

Name	Email	in ⬚ f ✖	Phone/Cell

Name	Email	in ⬚ f ✖	Phone/Cell

Important Contacts

Name	Email	in ◻ f ▾	Phone/Cell

U.S. Customary Measures and Weights

Length					
1 inch	=	1000 mils	1 furlong	=	40 rods
1 foot	=	12 inches	1 statute mile	=	8 furlongs
1 yard	=	3 feet	1 statute mile	=	5280 feet
1 fathom	=	6 feet	1 nautical mile	=	6076 feet
1 rod	=	5 1/2 yards	1 league	=	3 miles

Area		
1 sq. foot	=	1 sq. inches
1 sq. yard	=	9 sq. feet
1 sq. rod	=	30 1/4 sq. yards
1 acre	=	160 sq. rods
1 acre	=	43,560 sq. ft.
1 sq. mile	=	640 acres

Dry Capacity					
2 pints	=	1 quart	=	67.2 cu. in.
8 quarts	=	1 peck	=	537.6 cu. in.
4 pecks	=	1 bushel	=	2150.4 cu. in.

Liquid Capacity		
1 gill	=	4 fluid ounces
1 pint	=	4 gills
1 quart	=	2 pints
1 gallon	=	4 quarts
1 barrel	=	31 1/2 gallons
1 hogshead	=	2 bbl. (63 gal)
1 tun	=	252 gallons
1 barrel (petrol)	=	42 gallons

Avoirdupois Weight				
1 dram	=	27.34 grains		
1 ounce	=	16 drams		
1 pound	=	16 ounces		
1 quarter	=	25 pounds		
1 short ton	=	2000 pounds		
1 long ton	=	2240 pounds		
1 lb avdp.	=	7000 grains	=	453.59 grains
		1.2153 lb. troy	=	1.2153 lb. apoth
1 grain	=	1 grain troy	=	1 grain apoth

Metric equivalents of U.S. Customary Measures and Weights

Length					
centi meter	=	0.3937 in.	inch	=	2.5400 cm.
meter	=	3.281 ft	ft	=	0.3048 m.
meter	=	1.0936 yard	yard	=	0.9144 m.
kilo meter	=	0.6214 mile	mile	=	1.6093 km.

Area		
sq. cm	=	0.1550 sq. inches
sq. m.	=	10.764 sq. ft
sq. km.	=	0.3861 sq. mile
sq. in.	=	6.4516 sq. cm.
sq. ft.	=	0.0929 sq. m.
sq. mile	=	2590 sq. ft.

Capacity		
liter	=	61.024 cu. in.
liter	=	0.0353 cu. ft
liter	=	0.2642 gal. (US)
liter	=	0.0284 bu. (US)
liter	=	1000 cu. cm.
liter	=	1.0567 qt. (liquid) or 0.9081 qt. (dry)
liter	=	2.2046 lb. of pure water at 4 deg C = 1 kg.
cu. in.	=	0.0164 liter
cu. ft.	=	28.32 liters
gal.	=	3.785 liters
bu.	=	35.24 liters

Weight		
gram	=	15.4324 grains
gram	=	0.03532 oz. avdp.
kg.	=	2.2046 lb. avdp.
kg.	=	0.00110 ton (sht)
grain	=	0.0648 g.
oz. avdp	=	28.35 g.
lb. avdp.	=	0.4536 kg.
ton (sht)	=	907.2 kg.

Volume		
cu. cm.	=	0.06102 cu. in.
cu. m.	=	35.31 cu. ft.
cu. in.	=	16.387 cu. cm.
cu. ft.	=	0.02832 cu. m.

Pressure		
kg. per sq. cm.	=	14.223 lb. per sq. in.
lb. per sq. in.	=	0.0703 kg. per sq. cm.
kg. per sq. m.	=	0.2048 lb. per sq. ft.
lb. per sq. ft.	=	4.882 kg. per sq. m.
kg. per sq. cm.	=	0.9679 normal atm.
normal atm.	=	1.0332 kg. per sq. cm.
normal atm.	=	1.0133 bars
normal atm.	=	14.696 lb. per sq. in.
pascals	=	0.000145 lb. per sq. in.
megapascals	=	145 lb. per sq. in.
lb. per sq. in.	=	6894.7 pascals
atm.		atmosphere